**HAL LEONARD**

 *MORE* **EASY BANJO SOLOS**

BY MAC ROBERTSON

Welcome to *More Easy Banjo Solos*, a collection of 16 timeless songs arranged for 5-string banjo. This beginner's songbook can be used on its own or as a supplement to the *Hal Leonard Banjo Method*, or any other beginning banjo method. The songs are arranged in order of difficulty and presented in an easy-to-follow format.

The author gratefully acknowledges Jon Peik's assistance with arrangements.

ISBN 978-0-7935-2688-8

 **HAL•LEONARD®**
CORPORATION
7777 W. BLUEMOUND RD. P.O. BOX 13819 MILWAUKEE, WI 53213

Visit Hal Leonard Online at
www.halleonard.com

JAMBALAYA
(On the Bayou)

Words and Music by
Hank Williams

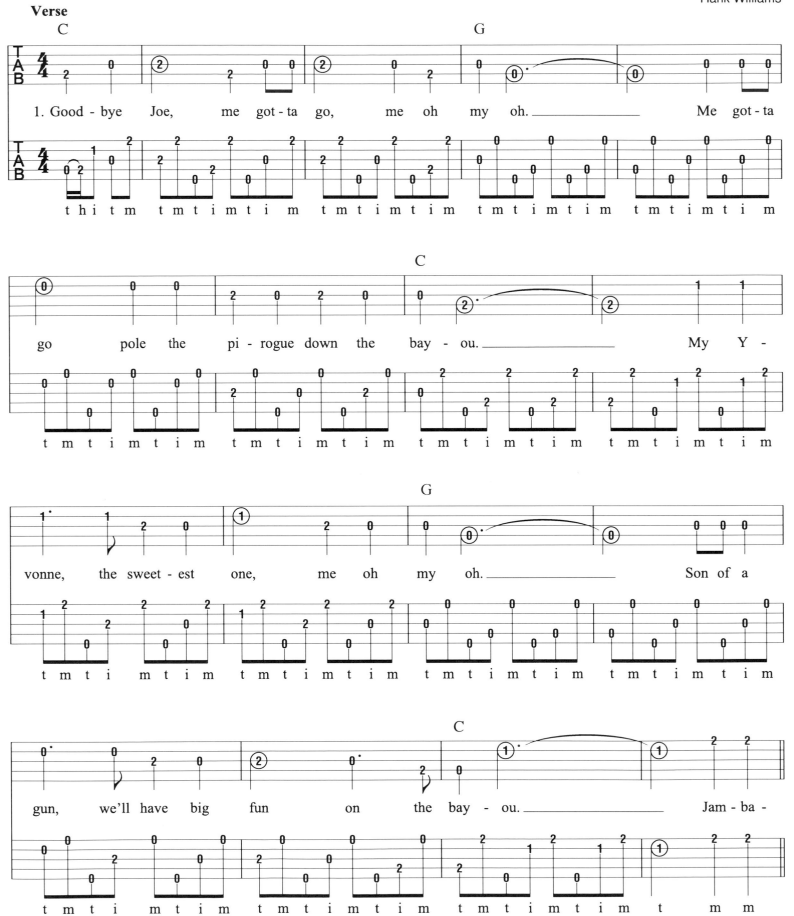

Chorus

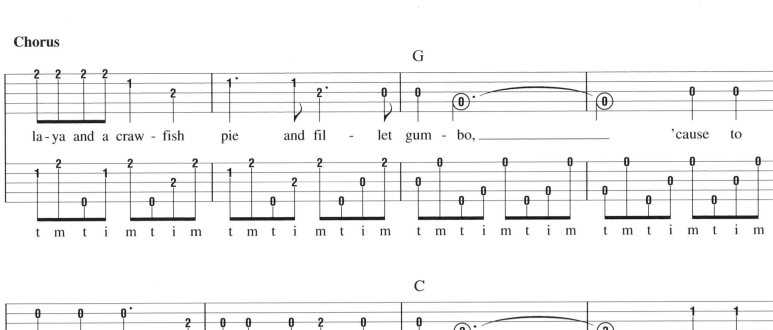

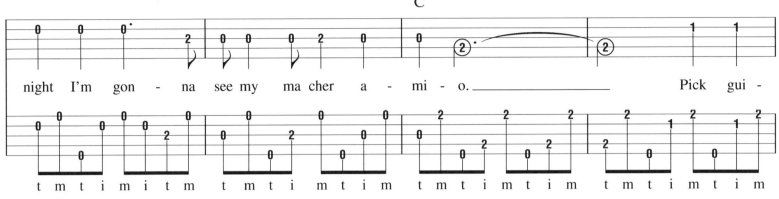

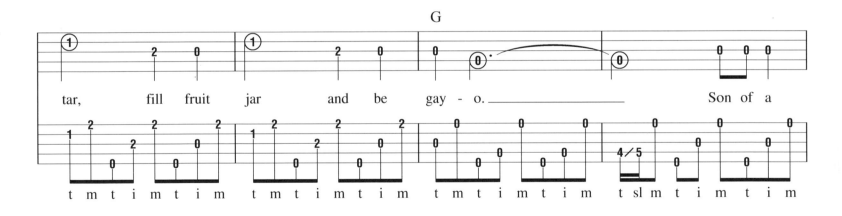

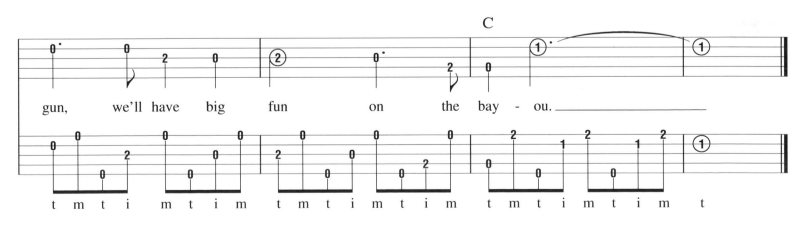

Additional Verse

2. Thibodaux, Fontaineaux the place is buzzin',
   Kinfolk come to see Yvonne by the dozen.
   Dress in style and go hog wild, me oh my oh.
   Son of a gun we'll have big fun on the bayou. *CHORUS*

CORNBREAD AND BUTTER BEANS

Words and Music by Dominique Flemons,
Rhiannon Giddens Laffan and Thomas Justin Robinson

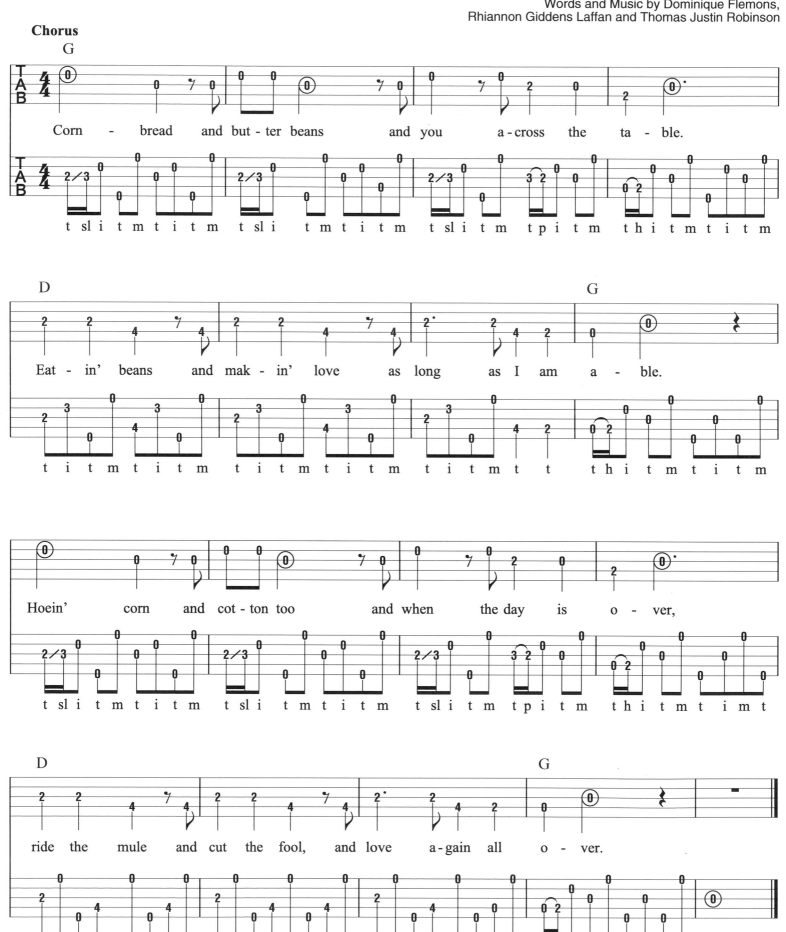

YOUR LOVE IS LIKE A FLOWER

By E. Lilly, Lester Flatt and Earl Scruggs

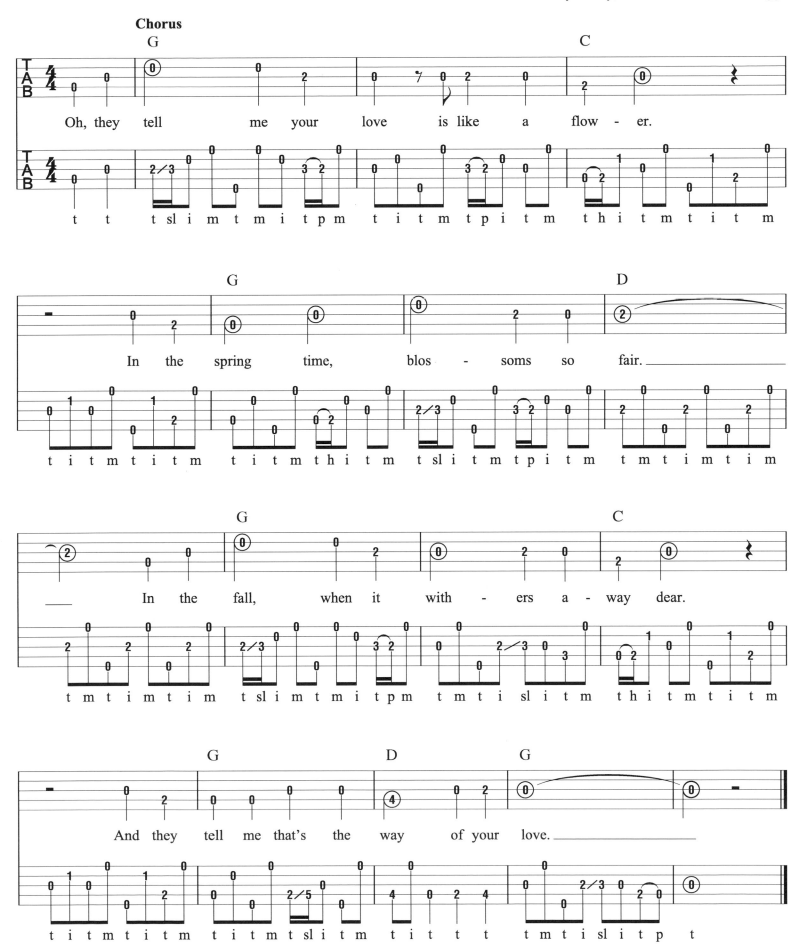

BIG SANDY RIVER

By Bill Monroe and Kenny Baker

denotes a triplet rhythm. The basic quarter note beat is divided into three equal notes.

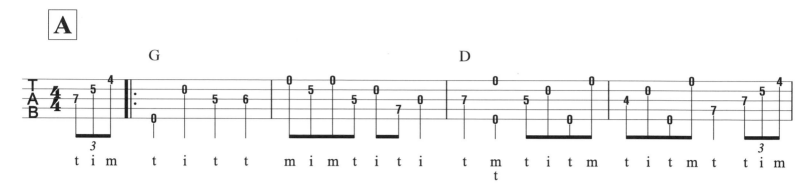

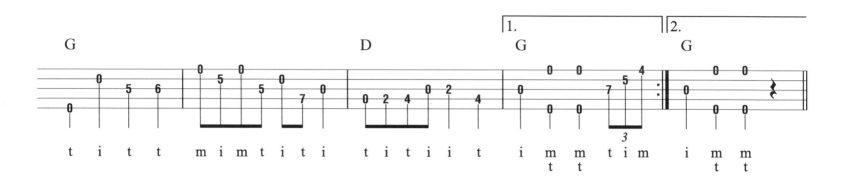

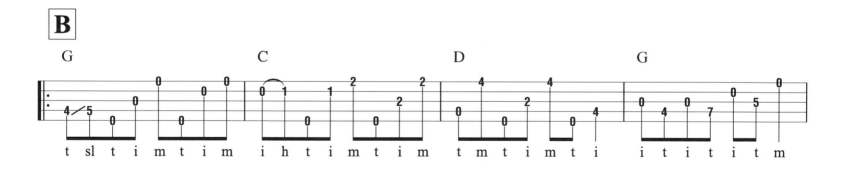

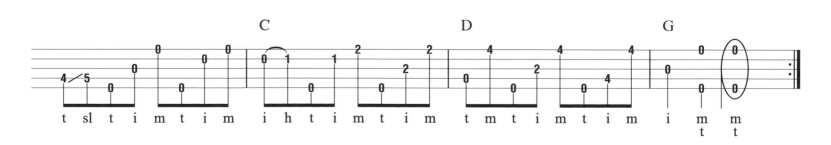

I'M SO LONESOME I COULD CRY

Words and Music
by Hank Williams

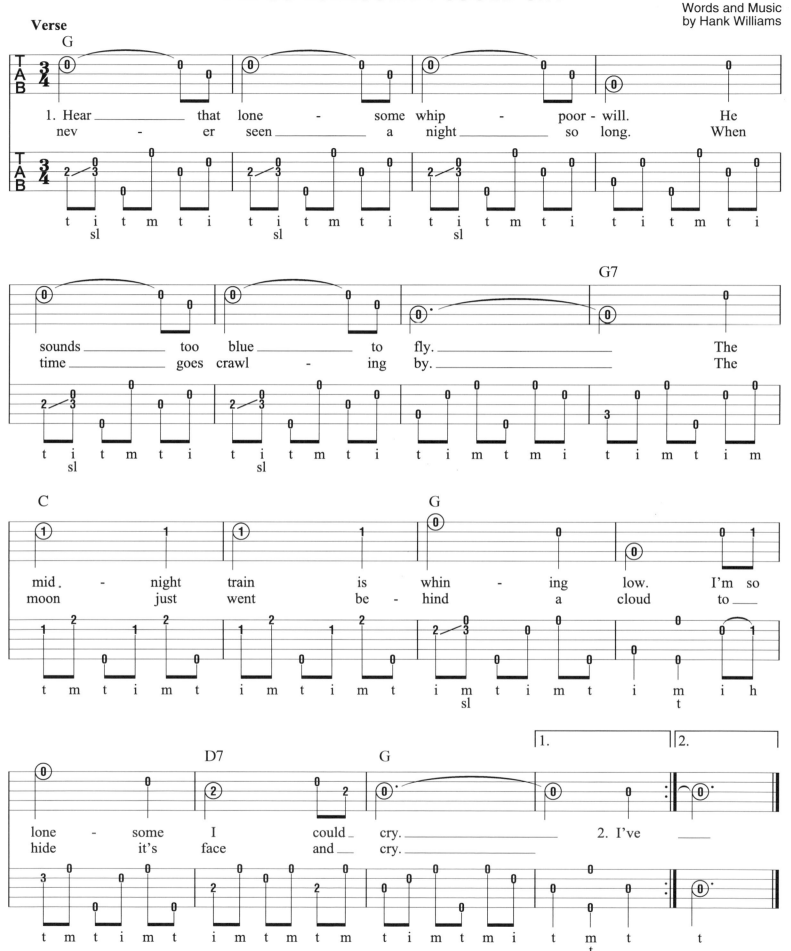

I AM A MAN OF CONSTANT SORROW

Words and Music by
Carter Stanley

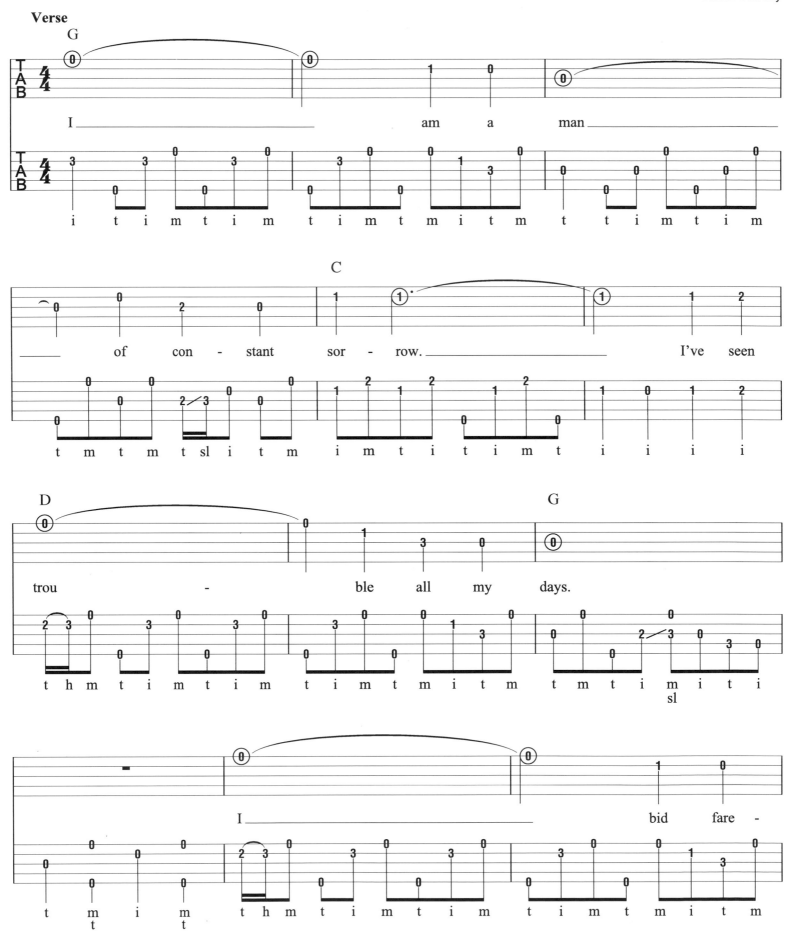

8

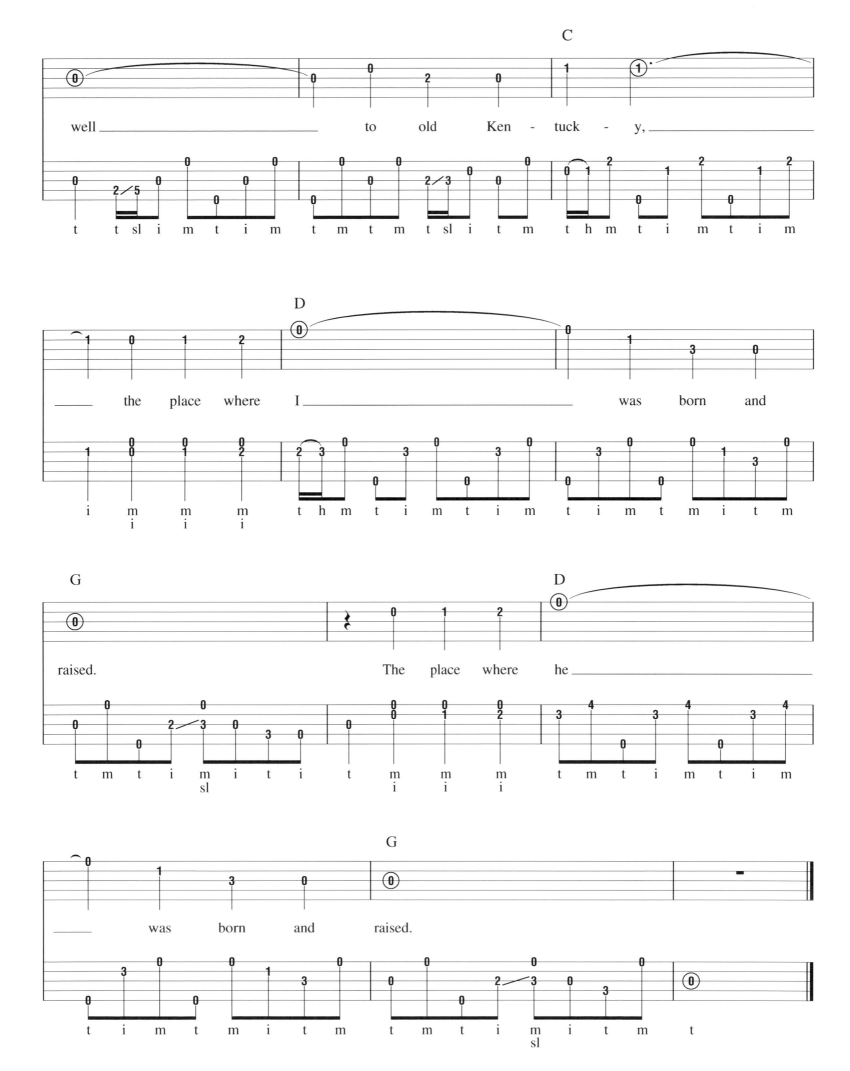

ABILENE

Words and Music by Lester Brown,
John D. Loudermilk and Bob Gibson

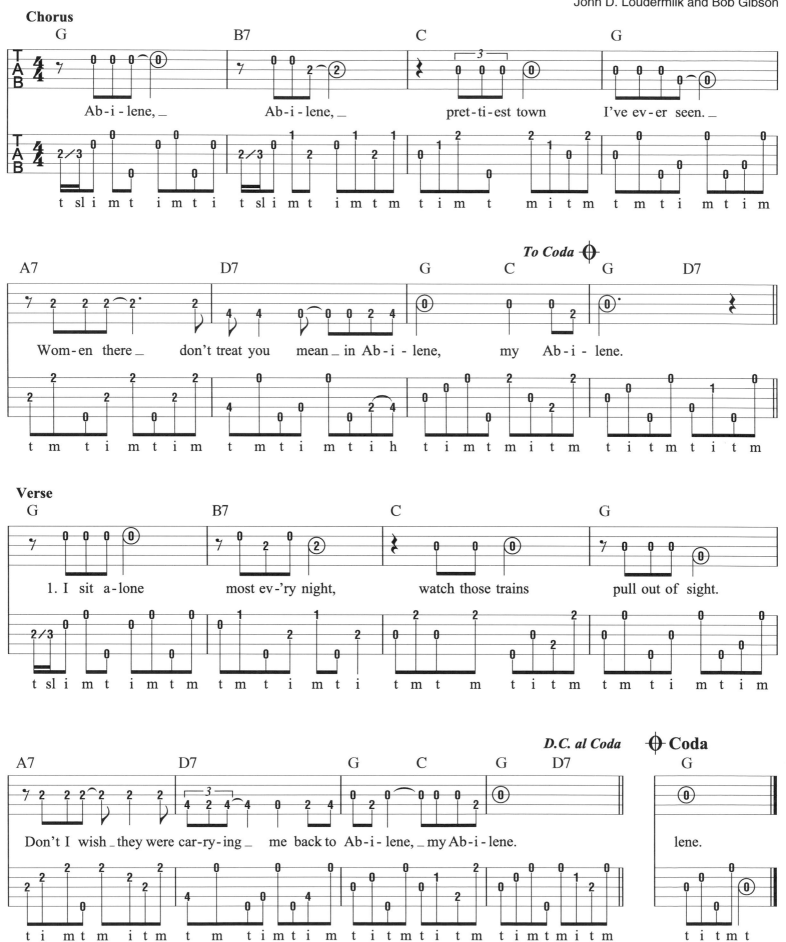

FREIGHT TRAIN

Words and Music by
Elizabeth Cotten

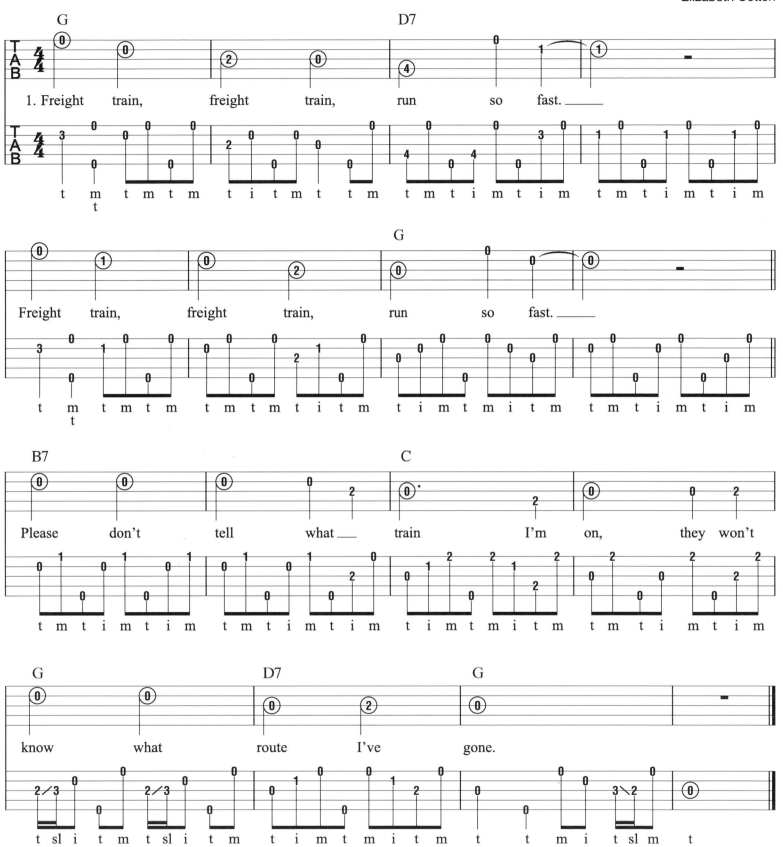

Additional Verses

2. When I'm dead and in my grave,
   No more good times here I'll crave.
   Place the stones at my head and feet
   And tell them I've gone to sleep.

3. When I die, Lord, bury me deep,
   Way down on old Chestnut Street,
   So I can hear old Number Nine
   As she comes rolling by.

WORDS UNSPOKEN

Words and Music by Steve Martin
and Peter Wernick

Open D Tuning:
*(5th-1st) A-D-F#-A-D

A

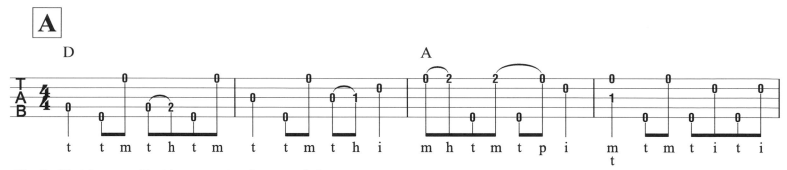

*For the 5th string, use a 5th-string capo or tune it up one whole step.

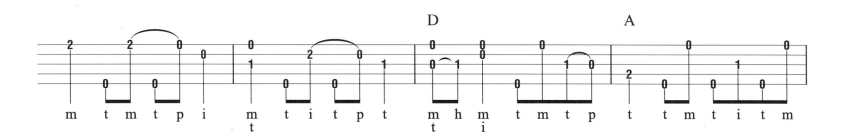

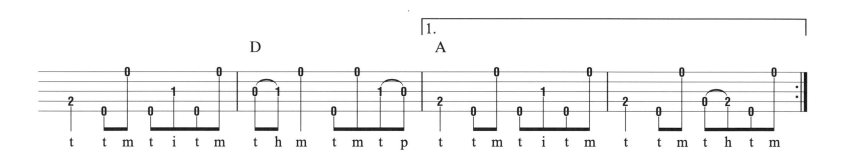

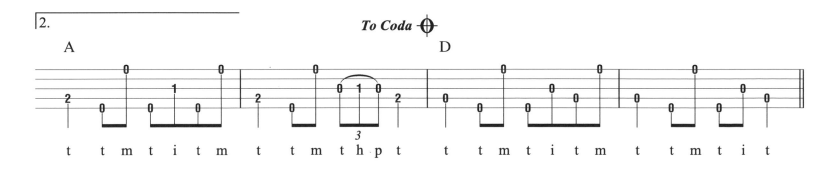

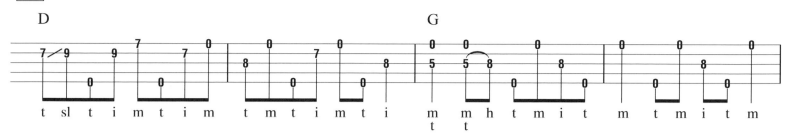

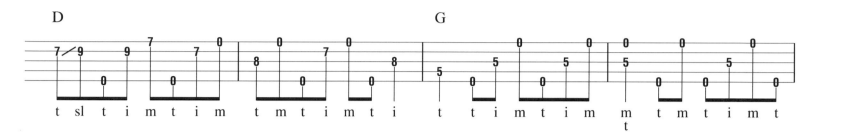

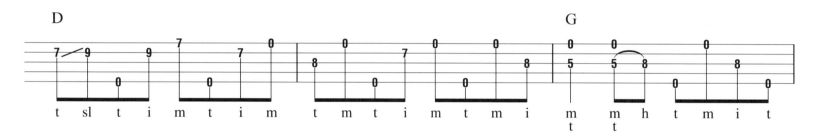

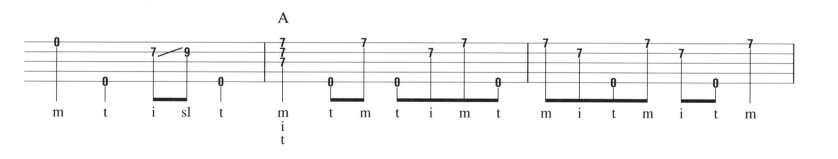

D.C. al Coda
(take repeat)

⊕ **Coda**

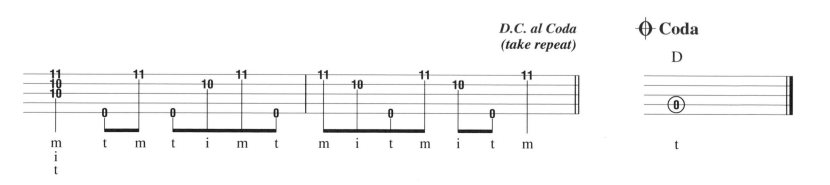

DOUG'S TUNE
(My Grass Is Blue)

Words and Music by
Douglas Dillard

Place the left hand fingers in this pattern to begin the song:

213

At measure three use this fingering:

3

Reminder: indicates a fret hand pull-off.

indicates that the notes are tied together.

A

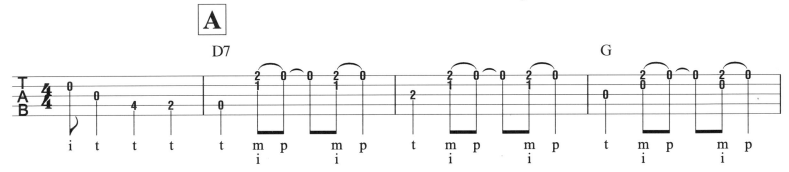

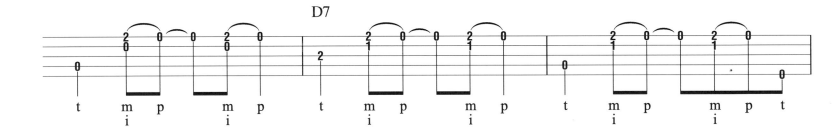

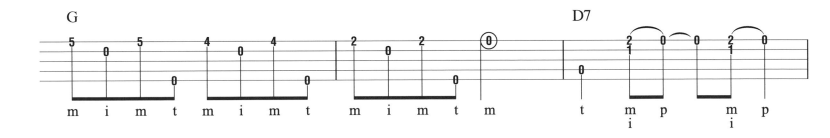

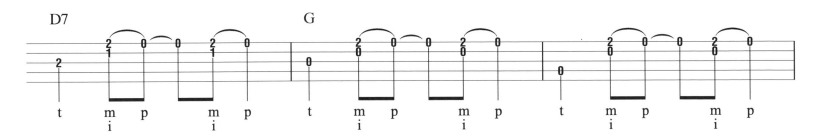

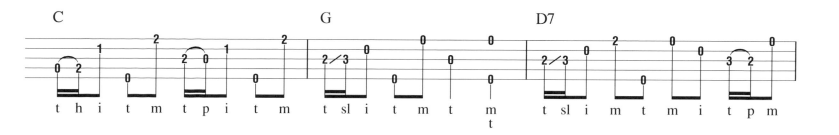

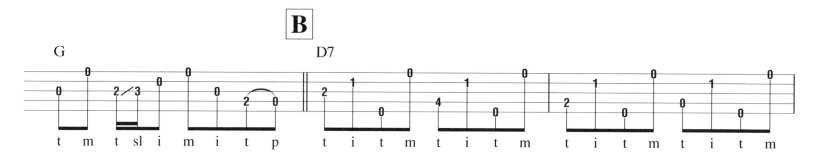

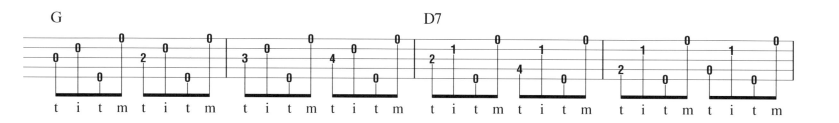

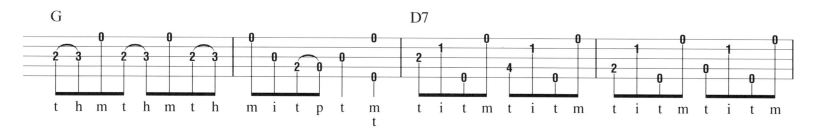

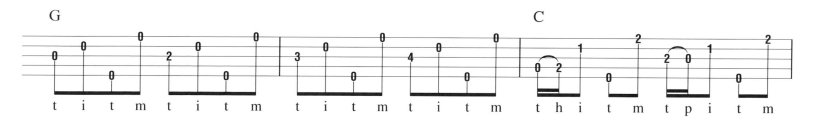

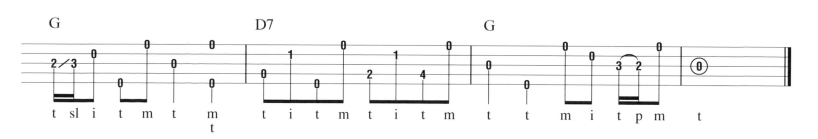

RED WING

Words by Thurland Chattaway
Music by Kerry Mills

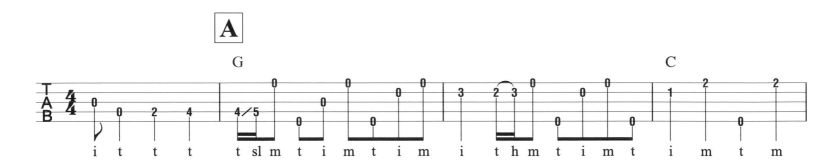

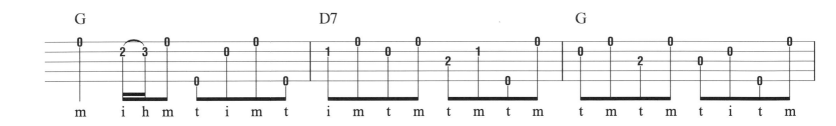

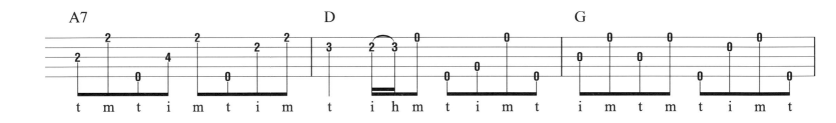

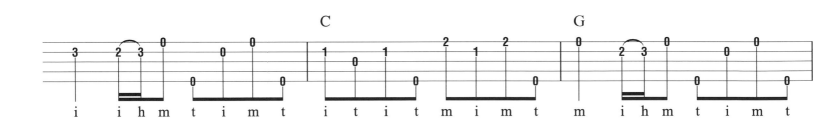

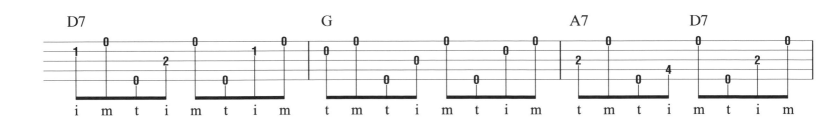

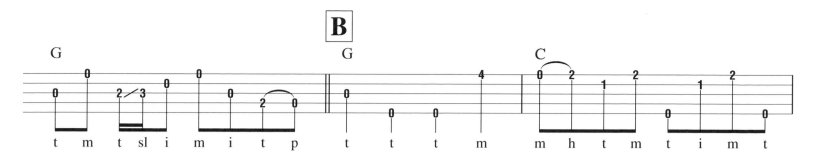

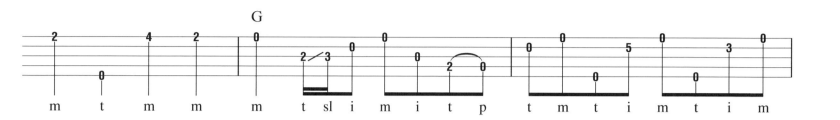

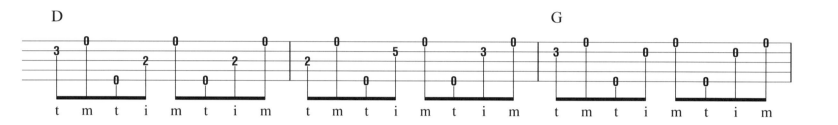

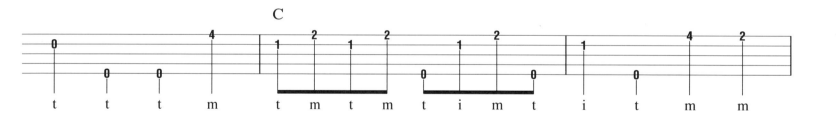

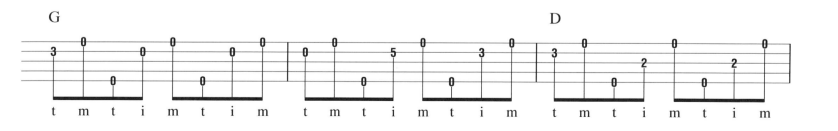

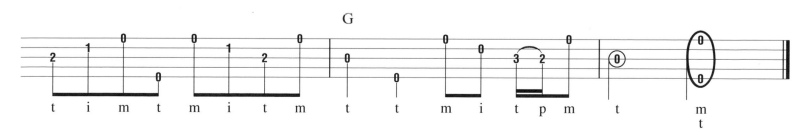

BLACKBERRY BLOSSOM

Traditional

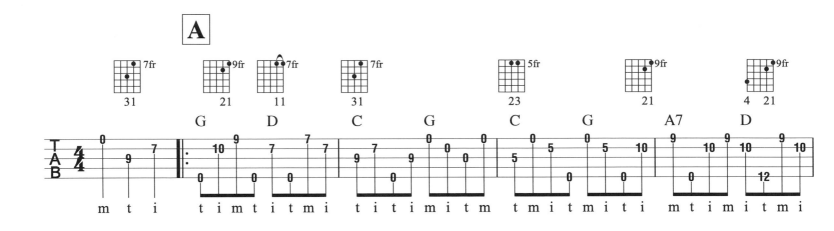

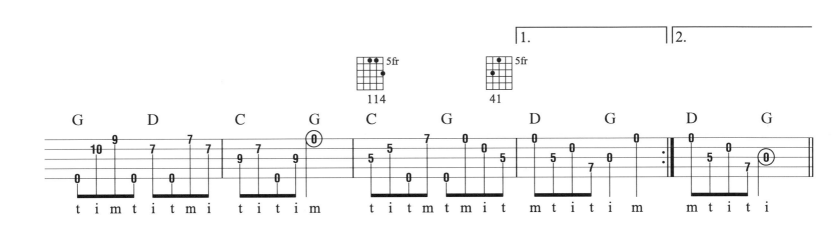

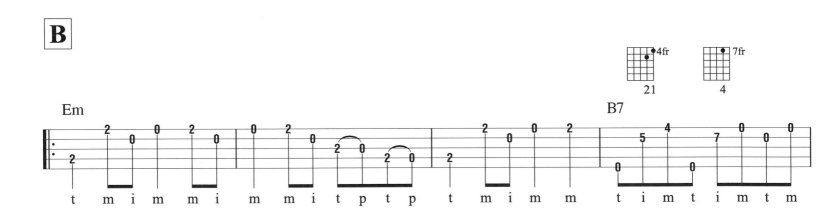

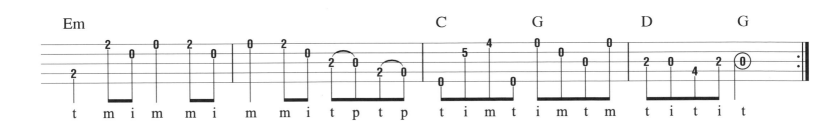

BLUE MOON OF KENTUCKY

Words and Music by
Bill Monroe

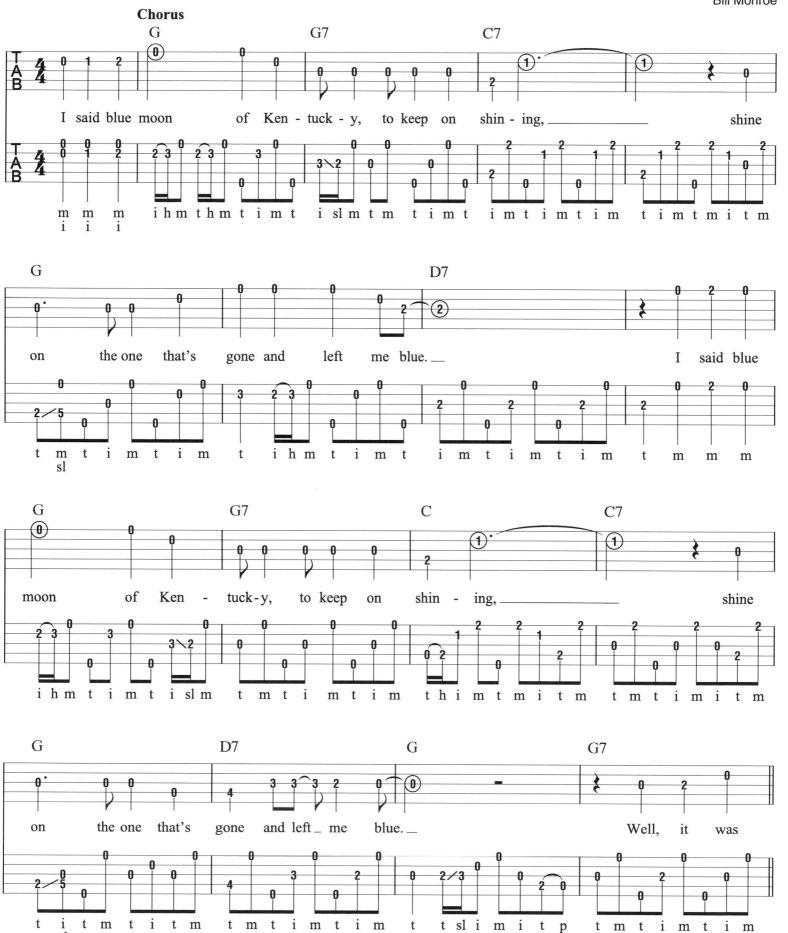

Bridge

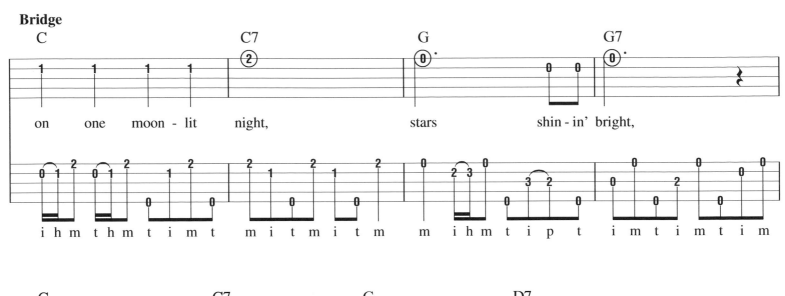

on one moon - lit night, stars shin - in' bright,

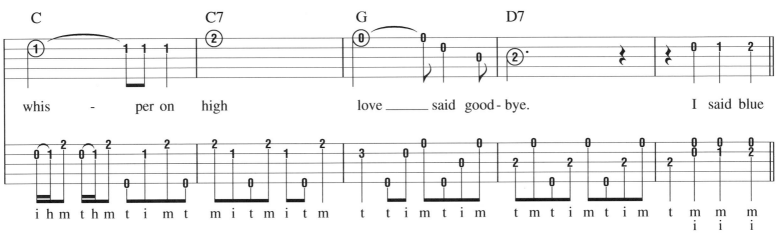

whis - per on high love _____ said good - bye. I said blue

Chorus

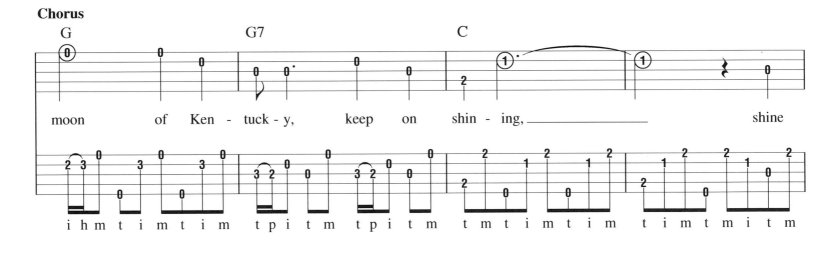

moon of Ken - tuck - y, keep on shin - ing, _____ shine

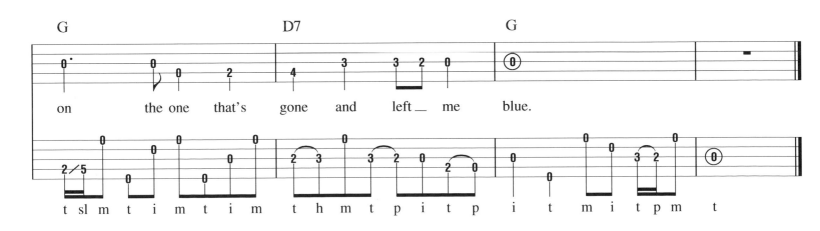

on the one that's gone and left __ me blue.

SALTY DOG BLUES

Words and Music by Wiley A. Morris
and Zeke Morris

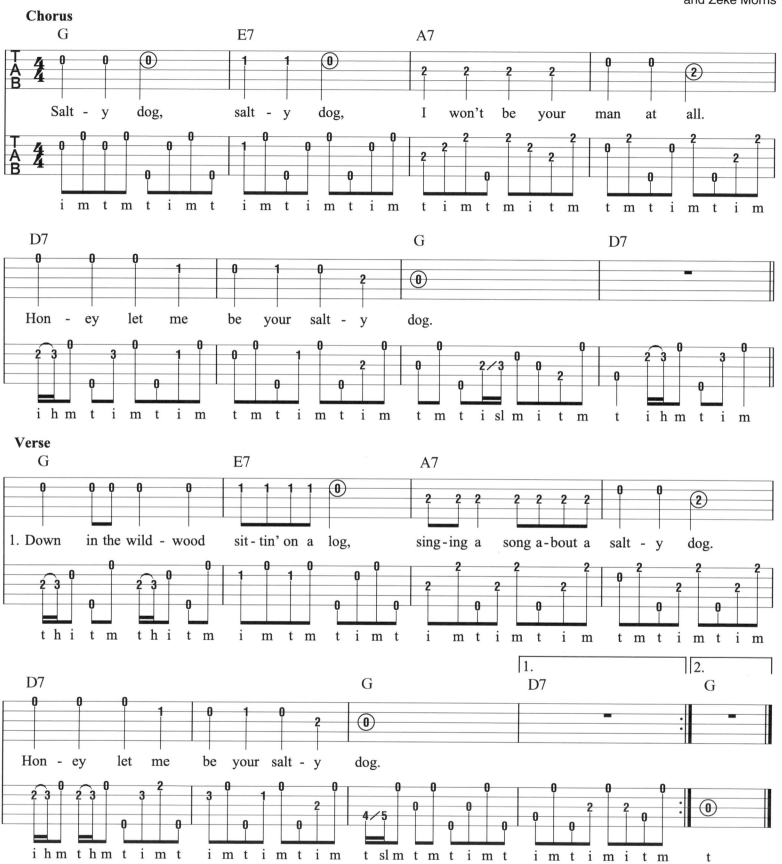

Additional Verses

2. I was down in the henhouse on my knees
Thought I heard a chicken sneeze.
Honey let me be your salty dog.

3. It was only the rooster sayin' his prayers
Thankin' the Lord for the hens upstairs.
Honey let me be your salty dog.

Foggy Mountain Breakdown

By Earl Scruggs

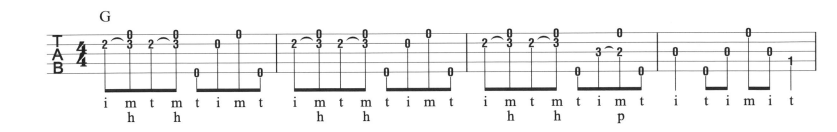

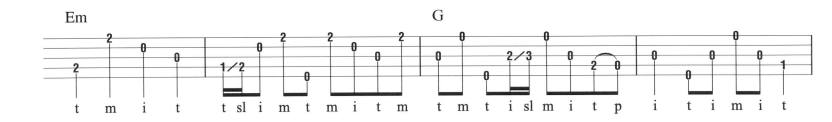

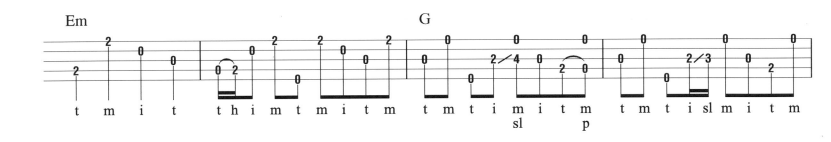

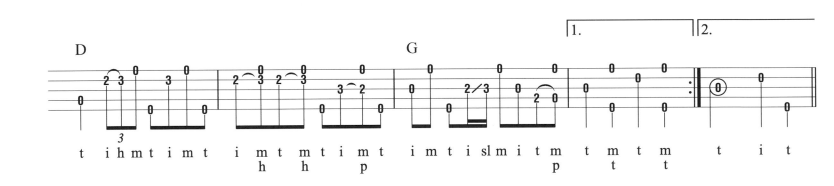

Tag Ending:

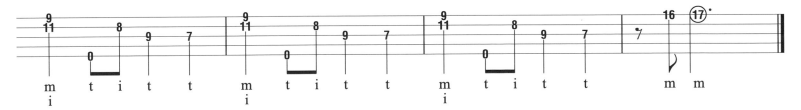

TEMPERENCE REEL

Traditional

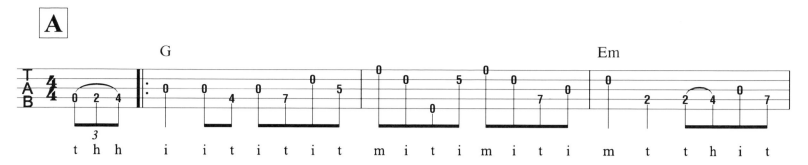

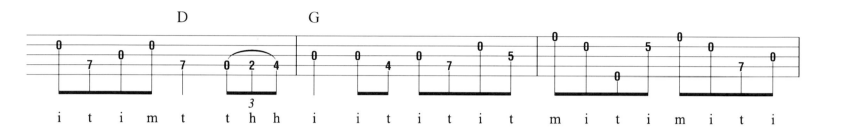

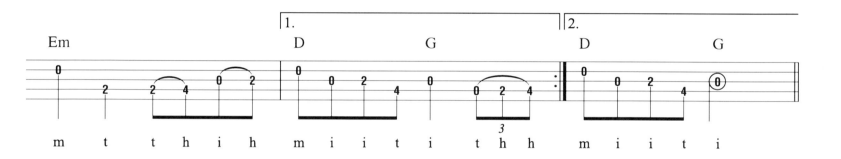

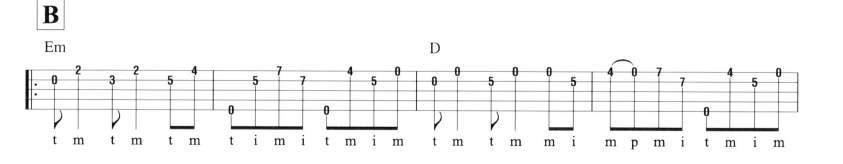

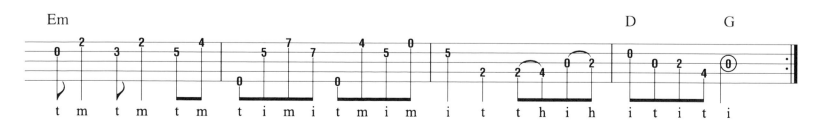

GREAT BANJO PUBLICATIONS

FROM HAL LEONARD

Hal Leonard Banjo Method – Second Edition
by Mac Robertson, Robbie Clement, Will Schmid
This innovative method teaches 5-string banjo bluegrass style using a carefully paced approach that keeps beginners playing great songs *while learning*. Book 1 covers easy chord strums, tablature, right-hand rolls, hammer-ons, slides and pull-offs, and more. Book 2 includes solos and licks, fiddle tunes, back-up, capo use, and more.
00699500 Book 1 Book Only $7.99
00695101 Book 1 Book/Online Audio $16.99
00699502 Book 2 Book Only $7.99

Banjo Aerobics
A 50-Week Workout Program for Developing, Improving and Maintaining Banjo Technique
by Michael Bremer
Take your banjo playing to the next level with this fantastic daily resource, providing a year's worth of practice material with a two-week vacation. The accompanying audio includes demo tracks for all the examples in the book to reinforce how the banjo should sound.
00113734 Book/Online Audio $19.99

Banjo Chord Finder
This extensive reference guide covers over 2,800 banjo chords, including four of the most commonly used tunings. Thirty different chord qualities are covered for each key, and each chord quality is presented in two different voicings. Also includes a lesson on chord construction and a fingerboard chart of the banjo neck!
00695741 9 x 12.................. $8.99   00695742 6 x 9...................... $6.99

Banjo Scale Finder
by Chad Johnson
Learn to play scales on the banjo with this comprehensive yet easy-to-use book. It contains more than 1,300 scale diagrams for the most often-used scales and modes, including multiple patterns for each scale. Also includes a lesson on scale construction and a fingerboard chart of the banjo neck.
00695780 9 x 12.................. $9.99   00695783 6 x 9...................... $6.99

First 50 Songs You Should Play on Banjo
arr. Michael J. Miles & Greg Cahill
Easy-to-read banjo tab, chord symbols and lyrics for the most popular songs banjo players like to play. Explore clawhammer and three-finger-style banjo in a variety of tunings and capoings with this one-of-a-kind collection. Songs include: Angel from Montgomery • Carolina in My Mind • Cripple Creek • Danny Boy • The House of the Rising Sun • Mr. Tambourine Man • Take Me Home, Country Roads • This Land Is Your Land • Wildwood Flower • and many more.
00153311 ....$14.99

Fretboard Roadmaps
by Fred Sokolow
This handy book/with online audio will get you playing all over the banjo fretboard in any key! You'll learn to: increase your chord, scale and lick vocabulary • play chord-based licks, moveable major and blues scales, melodic scales and first-position major scales • and much more! The audio includes 51 demonstrations of the exercises.
00695358 Book/Online Audio $15.99

O Brother, Where Art Thou?
Banjo tab arrangements of 12 bluegrass/folk songs from this Grammy-winning album. Includes: The Big Rock Candy Mountain • Down to the River to Pray • I Am a Man of Constant Sorrow • I Am Weary (Let Me Rest) • I'll Fly Away • In the Jailhouse Now • Keep on the Sunny Side • You Are My Sunshine • and more, plus lyrics and a banjo notation legend.
00699528 Banjo Tablature........................... $14.99

Earl Scruggs and the 5-String Banjo
Earl Scruggs' legendary method has helped thousands of banjo players get their start. It features everything you need to know to start playing, even how to build your own banjo! Topics covered include: Scruggs tuners • how to read music • chords • how to read tablature • anatomy of Scruggs-style picking • exercises in picking • 44 songs • biographical notes • and more! The online audio features Earl Scruggs playing and explaining over 60 examples!
00695764 Book Only................................. $24.99
00695765 Book/Online Audio................................. $34.99

Clawhammer Cookbook
Tools, Techniques & Recipes for Playing Clawhammer Banjo
by Michael Bremer
The goal of this book isn't to tell you how to play tunes or how to play like anyone else. It's to teach you ways to approach, arrange, and personalize any tune – to develop your own unique style. To that end, we'll take in a healthy serving of old-time music and also expand the clawhammer palate to taste a few other musical styles. Includes audio track demos of all the songs and examples to aid in the learning process.
00118354 Book/Online Audio..$19.99

The Ultimate Banjo Songbook
A great collection of banjo classics: Alabama Jubilee • Bye Bye Love • Duelin' Banjos • The Entertainer • Foggy Mountain Breakdown • Great Balls of Fire • Lady of Spain • Orange Blossom Special • (Ghost) Riders in the Sky • Rocky Top • San Antonio Rose • Tennessee Waltz • UFO-TOFU • You Are My Sunshine • and more.
00699565 Book/Online Audio................................. $27.50

HAL•LEONARD®

Prices, contents, and availability subject to change without notice.